D1080058

DISCOVER
ROBOTICS

First published 2020 by North Parade Publishing Limited
4 North Parade
Bath
BA1 1LF, UK

Predominant artwork and imagery source: Shutterstock. com, Atlas Robot, Spot Robot and Handle Robot images courtesy of Boston Dynamics. Other company sources: Reach Robotics, Sphero, Spin Master, Open Bionics, ANKI, Small Robot Company, Festo and Rovco.

Printed in China.

Contents

An Introduction to Robotics

Robotics, in simple terms, is the use of intelligent machines or 'robots' to help humans perform manual tasks. If robots do all the dull, dangerous and dirty work for us, our lives can be more productive and enjoyable. At home, robots are beginning to take on household chores, helping us study and being companion for play. In factories, robots are helping more and more companies manufacture and supply products. As robotic technology improves and combines with artificial intelligence, robots are finding more useful applications.

Robots do not need to resemble a human: in fact, they can be any shape or size. However, androids are specific robots that are designed to look and act exactly like a human, so are always humanoid.

Robots are most likely to have some physical likeness to living beings or at least replicate something that living things do, in order to be thought of as more than just a software programme, a computer or a machine.

Myths and science fiction have given us ideas of what robots might become in the future. Here are a few examples of charismatic robots from famous films. Do you recognise them?

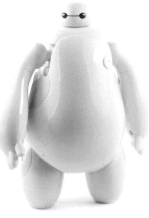

What makes these robots more appealing and memorable are their personalities, but in truth robots do not start with any character: it is programmed into them, just like a mobile app, game or software programme is programmed to behave in a certain way. Due to the physical presence of robots alongside sophisticated programming, cameras and sensors for facial recognition, a lot can be achieved to create appealing characters that appear to know you and your behaviour. These robots are often designed to grow in depth and knowledge over time. We'll see real-life examples of these types of robots later in the book and look in more detail at the topic of robots' brains through programming, control and artificial intelligence (AI).

The Origins of Robotics

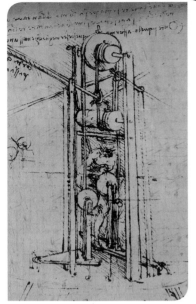

The desire for humans to create moving life-like forms can be seen as far back as 25,000 years ago with evidence of statues with moving joints. The first machines were created by the Ancient Egyptians around 4000 years ago who used water to power clocks and these ideas have developed over the centuries to move us towards the robotic mechanisms we recognise today.

It was the Ancient Greeks who actually invented the first working robotic mechanisms over 2000 years ago, although the words 'robot' and 'robotics' weren't invented themselves until the last century. The Great Library of Alexandria in Greece was a centre point for science and invention at that time and its scholars Ktesibios, Philo and latterly Hero created a number of powered mechanisms that made animal and human forms appear as if they were moving on their own.

These self-operating machines became known as automatons which meant 'acting of one's own will'. We commonly use the derived words automatic and automation to mean fulfilling a task or process with little human intervention. When a robot is said to be autonomous, it means it is largely self-operating. Greek inventors brought us accurate clocks and crafted moving humans and animals powered through hot air, steam or water by using their mechanical ingenuity.

Hero's written illustrations in particular were an inspiration to scientists and inventors around the world over the next 1500 years. It was only with the invention of mechanical clocks that these other mechanical methods became outdated for automation. Around this time, approximately 500 years ago, Leonardo Da Vinci invented a mechanical knight, which is often referred to now as 'Leonardo's Robot'. The device was operated by pulleys and cables and could stand, sit, manoeuvre its arms and raise its own visor.

By the 17th Century self-operating machines had become quite sophisticated, made of complex moving pieces including gears, cams and wires, like the finest clocks of the day, and only affordable by the very rich. The intricacy of clockwork mechanisms increased with time and the best examples were built in Switzerland, France and Japan. A series of inventions in the past 150 years has advanced our aspirations for all technology and made robotics what it is today. The most significant of these innovations to robotics was electronics.

In 1927, Westinghouse, the most significant US technology company of the day, built the Televox robot, but as you can see in the picture, this was just a cardboard robot in front of a box of technology; but the race to show off a working electronic robot was truly on. Just a year later, W.H. Richards exhibited a working aluminium robot called Eric which was controlled by remote or voice commands and capable of moving its hands and head. The following year (1929) the first Japanese robot Gakutensoku was demonstrated to an amazed public.

The first electronic autonomous robots were created by William Grey Walter (1949), a scientist whose pair of small tortoise-like robots (called Elmer and Elsie) were designed to demonstrate and prove his theories of how the brain worked, particularly how simple systems of motors and sensors can have complex and unpredictable behaviours. In 1954, the first digitally operated and programmable robot was invented in the US by George Devol, called Unimate (from Universal Automation). This invention was the first robot to be used in car assembly and helped lay the foundations for industrial robots used in manufacturing today. The past fifty years have seen significant advances in computing and reductions in cost for complex sensors meaning we are now hitting a golden era for consumer robotics, where we can afford to buy robots capable of things we've only ever previously heard of in science fiction.

Mythology and Science Fiction

Humans have been fascinated with stories of artificial beings and helpers for thousands of years. In Greek mythology Hephaestus, the god of fire, created an 8 feet tall bronze man, Talos, that defended Crete from pirates and challenged Jason and the Argonauts when they landed there. Talos was the first known robot created in literature and featured in the Argonautica, an epic Greek poem by Apollonius Rhodius from the 3rd Century BC, almost 2500 years ago.

HEPHAESTUS

The Greeks therefore developed both the idea in fiction as well as in the first working robotic mechanisms that have helped make robots what they are today.

It wasn't just in Greece that these ideas were being formed; early concepts for robotics were being envisioned in stories and theatre across China to Israel and Egypt. Ideas from the writers and storytellers of the day fed the creativity of the crafters of puppets and masks to enrapture and inspire audiences of the time.

Edward S Ellis is credited with bringing the first clear robot man to a book, in 'The Steam Man of the Prairies' published in 1868. Having a robot powered by steam made a great deal of sense at a time when steam was the primary engine type for powering machines in factories, trains and boats.

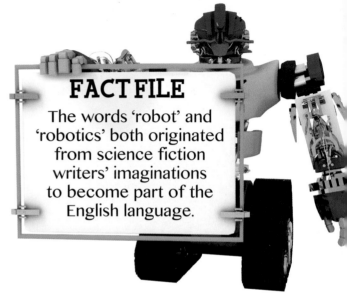

FACT FILE
The words 'robot' and 'robotics' both originated from science fiction writers' imaginations to become part of the English language.

In 1900, L. Frank Baum wrote 'The Wonderful Wizard of Oz', in which he told the story of a wood cutter who had his head, body, arms and legs replaced by bionic tin equivalents, he was just missing a heart. Baum continued his metal-man theme in other Oz books and created another early concept for a robot with his character Tik-Tok, a clockwork robot.

It wasn't until after 1920 that the term 'robot' was introduced by translating the Czech word robota, meaning 'forced labour" into English. It featured in Karel Čapek's play R.U.R. an acronym for Rossum's Universal Robots. His story envisaged manufactured artificial workers who looked human, remembered everything they were told, but thought of nothing new. It makes sense why this word was also used for programmable robots that follow a set of commands to automate factory work.

Metropolis was one of the first films to portray a robot on screen. This German film (1926) introduced the Maschinenmensch (which translates as machine-human) to cinema audiences. This creation was a metallic android who took her personality from a female character. The physical appearance of this robot was a strong influence on many humanoid robot characters that followed, for example in science fiction television shows like Dr Who (Cybermen - image on left) and films including Star Wars (C-3PO).

I, Robot

The boundaries between science fiction and non-fiction can blur to such a degree, that either can inform the other and help shape ideas for technology. An example of this is American author Isaac Asimov, who was a university professor and a prolific writer of science fiction. His most famous publication is the collection of stories called I, Robot (1950). In these stories he coined the term Robotics, which we have adopted into mainstream use. He also contributed the Three Laws of Robotics (see below), which have endured as the fundamental set of ethical guidelines for all created beings, especially autonomous robots.

If you had to choose a single country most linked with robotics, this would be Japan. the 1950s Osamu Tezuka introduced the hugely popular cartoon and TV series Mighty Atom, which was popular around the world and called Astro Boy for English-speaking audiences. The main character is an android boy with human emotions, almost like a robot Pinocchio, created as a substitute for a real son. Robots were becoming an accepted norm in science fiction during the 1950s and 60s, at a time when humans were regularly being launched into space by Russia and America. The film Forbidden Planet (1956) had a central robot character called Robbie, who followed Asimov's robotic laws.

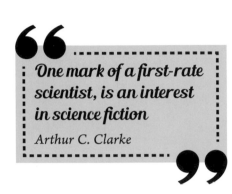

One mark of a first-rate scientist, is an interest in science fiction

Arthur C. Clarke

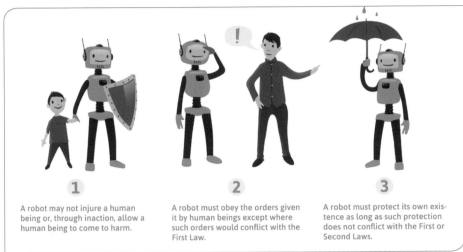

1 A robot may not injure a human being or, through inaction, allow a human being to come to harm.

2 A robot must obey the orders given it by human beings except where such orders would conflict with the First Law.

3 A robot must protect its own existence as long as such protection does not conflict with the First or Second Laws.

Lost in Space (1965) saw a space travelling family became lost due to a sabotaged robot, who destroyed vital parts of the spaceship's systems. Film makers have enjoyed exploring when robots contradict Asimov's laws and work against humans. Michael Crichton's Westworld film (1973) centres on a cowboy robot who malfunctions and starts shooting guests at a robotic theme world. Bladerunner's (1982) super-human androids escape slavery on Mars and violently seek answers from their creators on Earth. The Terminator (1984) stars Arnold Schwarzenegger as a time travelling android assassin trying to change the course of future events. In subsequent Terminator films, Schwarzenegger switches to the side of humanity to fight against an out of control AI system (Skynet) that decides the world would be a better place if humans didn't exist.

There are plenty of science fiction stories that give robots much more likeable human traits. For example Disney's WALL-E and Baymax from Big Hero 6 both exude positive characteristics, emotions and quirks which help make them truly endearing to an audience and a great ally to onscreen human characters. Star Trek (TV series and films) shows android crew members working side-by-side with human counterparts, their greater intelligence and strength is put to use for people's and humanity's benefit. Perhaps the best-known robot characters in science fiction are C-3PO and R2D2, the interplay between these two brings humour and a robotic camaraderie that continues through all the Star Wars films and we hope always does.

Robot Parts

Size and weight

A robot's shape and body plan are called its morphology. When a robot is being created, the designers need to know what the robot's function is; this helps their understanding of the components that need to work, which in turn also help govern its size. Another very important consideration is where it will be used, called its working environment. Some robots assume a human size and shape because they need to work in spaces where humans work, perhaps opening and fitting through doors or using our tools, but achieving human shape and function is extremely difficult and is almost never the best starting point to achieve an ideal robotic solution to a problem.

For example, if you need a robot to go into space and collect samples from Mars, with no direct human contact, considerations for safety or face-to-face communication with humans would not be a priority. More important considerations would be its strength and durability to survive the journey and its ability to perform tasks when on the Mar's surface. Though we see many humanoid robots on TV and in films, in reality most robots look nothing like humans. As you know, robots can be any size: you'll be amazed to know that nanorobots small enough to navigate within the blood in our bodies already exist to help fight cancer, and at the other end of the scale huge robot arms are helping to build aircraft in hangers every day.

Sensing

Just as we have five senses to help us make sense of the world around us, robots benefit from equivalents of these to interpret their environment. These senses are inputs to help a robot 'brain' understand what it needs to do. The good thing for robots is that they are not limited by five senses, in fact they can use numerous sensors and technology, for example to see in the dark.

If a robot is mobile it needs the equivalent of sight to move freely and avoid obstacles. The simplest sensor for this is a light sensor which can be used to help guide robots toward a light source and can also be used to judge distance. LIDAR uses laser light pulsed (quickly turned on and off) in known directions. The light that bounces back is accurately measured to help judge distances and interpret an environment. When linked with positional information (i.e. where you are on a map) LIDAR helps achieve safe navigation for robots and is also being used in connected autonomous vehicles (CAVs - see page 23).

Cameras on robots provide visual inputs to the robots to help give object and facial recognition, whilst AI and programming generally help the robot comprehend what it is seeing and tell it how to react to what it sees. Cameras are also essential when the robot is being tele-operated by a human. In a similar way to images from cameras, microphones and sound sensors are the inputs for sound including to help give a robot voice recognition. Touch for robots can come in the form of binary (on or off) sensors, to know if for example a button is pressed or not, alternatively, pressure, touch and proximity sensors can all give the robot an equivalent ability to judge if a wall or person is in front of it, for example. There are many more sensors that robots can adopt and use, for example to identify if an environment is safe for humans, and we will see more of these sensors in later parts of the book.

Intelligence

As mentioned on the first page, programming is an essential part of a robot's makeup and this can range from just a simple list of instructions to a very comprehensive set of behaviours. If your robot had no programming, you'd have a lot of expensive parts that wouldn't know how to respond to information coming from all its sensors. Intelligence in technology is and perhaps can only be artificial, as it is not naturally occurring and needs to be programmed in; however, the term artificial intelligence (AI) for robotics is more strongly associated with the aspiration for artificial general intelligence (AGI), which includes logical reasoning, problem solving and independent learning. AGI would give a robot seemingly natural and life-like intelligence. Other forms of AI are already widely used by robots alongside much computer driven technology to analyse and recognise data and information to achieve specific goals.

Locomotion

It isn't necessary for all robots to be mobile. For example, in a factory where products are being built, a robot arm is secured in a fixed position and moves around the objects it is working on. The products being made, for example cars, are typically carried to the robot arm on a conveyor belt. When a robot is mobile, its locomotion can take one of a few forms:

1) Moving along a fixed path or route guided by programming, a magnetic tape, barcodes, wire or rail. These are called Automatically Guided Vehicles (AGVs).

2) Teleoperated, like a remote-controlled car. A human operator, guided by direct sight or their view of the robot's perspective provided by cameras onboard the robot.

3) Free autonomous movement. This final type is the most difficult to achieve and requires an array of sensors and a lot of onboard intelligence to know or plan a route and avoid obstacles along the way.

Motors provide the drive for movement and traction with the surface achieved in a number of ways with a choice of tracks, legs and wheels, and of course robots can travel on or under water or in the air, as we will explore in the book.

Energy

How does the robot get the energy it needs to do what it needs to do? If the robot is fixed or has wired connections for communication and control, it is likely to have an additional wire to provide its power, since this will allow more continuous power than a battery or a renewable source of energy, (such as solar power or wind). An autonomous robots can still be tethered to a power source, but that link would limit its freedom of movement and restrict its distance for operation. Battery power allows more freedom, but with a finite charge and added weight, which is OK as long as the robot can perform its operation within the lifetime of the battery (before it needs recharging) and with the added weight.

Dexterity

Dexterity for robots is the equivalent of fine motor skills for humans, the movement and synchronisation of hands and fingers. Many robots, as you will see in the following pages, utilise tools to offer a means of interacting with the external environments and precise use is crucial to ensure, for example, a bomb is defused rather than triggered to explode or a car is assembled with absolute precision. As we will see in the section on bionics (see page 21), robotic arms can be a great substitute if you are missing a real one.

Communication & Control

Generally, computers and related input devices help humans tell a robot what they want it to do: in other words, control it. If the robot is close by, speech might be an ideal way to communicate, but perhaps not if you need to convey a lot of detailed co-ordinates and rules to follow. Generally, communication with a robot should be as easy and fast as possible.

In terms of outputs (how the robot tells humans information), these communications can be in the form of speech, lights or text and would take the form most useful for the interaction and environment. Communication with technology – verbal and nonverbal — is a large area of research within robotics. This area of work is called Human Robot Interaction (HRI).

Control devices can be wired or wireless, either programmed or human controlled. Industrial robots are mainly programmed by computer or pendant, consumer robots often by a mobile app.

Applications for Robotics

Social robots

Social robots are great communicators with humans They are the types of companion robots often envisioned in our future through science fiction, but they are already starting to be used in homes. Non-assistive social robots (i.e. ones that are directly trying to help you out in some way) are designed to be great company, often providing games and entertainment as well as being adorable pets. As you'll see in a few pages time, many of these types of toys now add an educational aspect alongside and during play.

Entertainment

Games

Companion

Fitness & Wellness

Education

Assistive social robots are built to help us out, they can also keep us connected and provide company and may be used by all age groups, from young to old. You will see social robots in any shape, but of all the categories you are most likely to see humanoid and androids robots designed for this area.

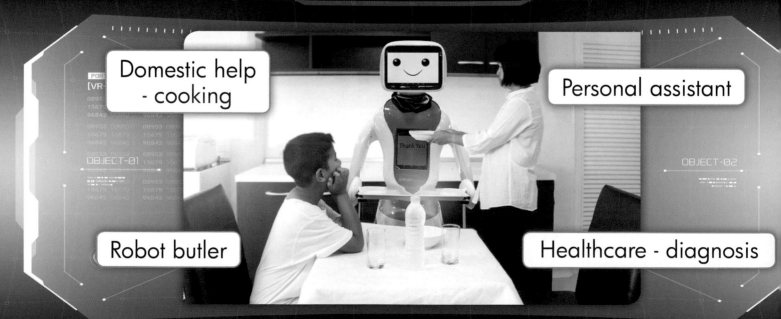

Domestic help - cooking

Personal assistant

Robot butler

Healthcare - diagnosis

Service robots

When robots are assisting us to take on chores that we find either too dull, dangerous or dirty, they are often categorised as service robots. There is a large amount of overlap between social and service robots as some service robots can be in a great deal of contact with humans, such as receptionists in hotels or theme parks. A service robot is less likely to have a single owner/user, compared with a social robot.

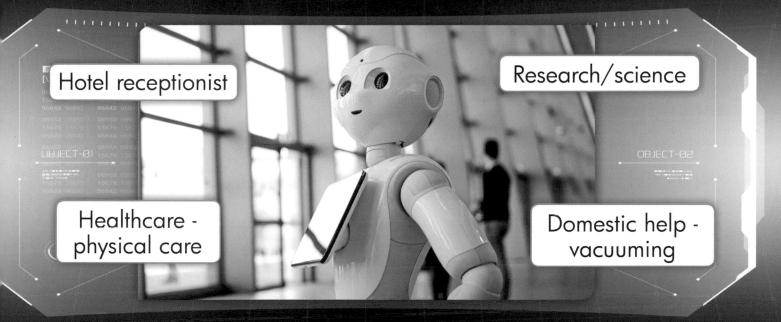

Hotel receptionist

Research/science

Healthcare - physical care

Domestic help - vacuuming

As service robots have more human contact than typical industrial robots they need to be extremely safe to be around, as well as being very easy to communicate with, typically with voice control and feedback.

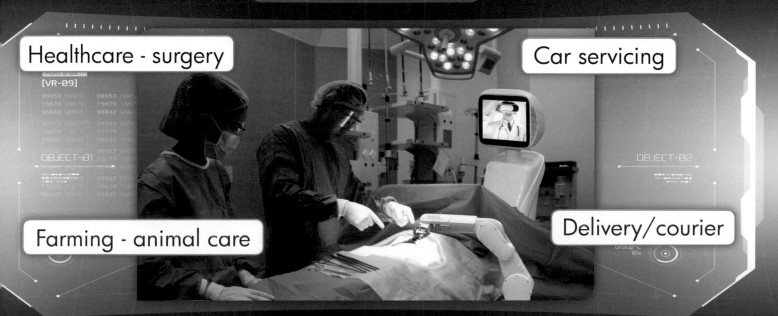

Healthcare - surgery

Car servicing

Farming - animal care

Delivery/courier

Industrial robots

Robotics is already a well-established, successful and growing product area for industrial uses. Robots provide a perfect solution for repetitive work that can keep going day and night. Imagine if you have to fit and tighten a bolt in one location on a thousand different cars every day. Most of us would find that incredibly dull; however robots, don't mind at all! Another strength of robots is that they can deal with conditions we'd struggle to work with, such as high temperatures, dangerous equipment and heavy weights. These kinds of robots tend not to work alongside humans and use articulated arms (manipulators) with tools to accomplish specific jobs. Control is given through programming to tell them clearly and precisely what to do.

Car manufacturing – welding & painting

Electronics assembly

The robot below is called Handle and adds mobility in small spaces, with legs or wheels, combined with a strong lifting arm. This robotic 'big-bird' was designed for stacking goods in warehouses. Some mobile robots or Automatic Guided Vehicles (AGVs) look more like cabinets on wheels or a small train with no driver, but that's the best design for the moving jobs they need to do.

Sort and pick – online retailers

Driverless storage trucks/carriers

Retail fulfilment systems

Unmanned lifting

Pallet stacking

Air - Drones or UAVs

Extreme environments

A remote-controlled vehicle that does tasks we'd rather not do (see below) tends to be called a robot. Similarly, if you use drones to do work, rather than fly them for fun, then these can be thought of as flying robots or unmanned aerial vehicles (UAVs). The work done by these drones is generally observation and information gathering, but they have also been trialled by online retailers delivering packages. Drones can achieve tasks that would previously have been very difficult, costly and time consuming – such as surveying and inspecting tall buildings to find a possible water leak.

Drones can also be deployed in military settings for intelligence gathering and are also used as remote-controlled or guided missiles. A far more positive and life-saving use for robotics is when they help disarm improvised explosive devices (IEDs). These tele-operated robots allow the operator to be at a safe distance away from the bomb when controlling it. Other key features of these robots are high resolution cameras to be able to see exactly what they are dealing with and a very dexterous and strong hand tool to manipulate wires and move the bomb if needed. Very similar robots are also used to inspect or move radioactive waste, which would otherwise mean people taking risks of exposure to radioactivity.

Bomb disposal

If that radioactive waste is underwater, it's possible to use either subsea robots called remotely operated underwater vehicles (ROVs) or autonomous underwater vehicles (AUVs). However, these robots are more commonly used for surveying large underwater areas to judge the potential for building oil or gas rigs or offshore renewable power (tidal or wind) generators or for scientific studies and ongoing monitoring. ROVs can also play a role in underwater security, either patrolling harbours or valuable boats.

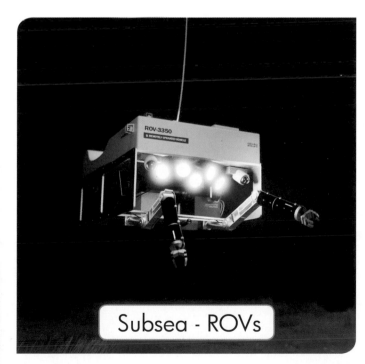

Subsea - ROVs

The final extreme environment, which probably couldn't be harsher, is space. It makes sense to send robots to far away planets instead of risking people's lives. Other advantages are that robots don't need food and they aren't worried about returning home either, so can stay in space forever. We get into more detail about these topics later in the book.

Planetary exploration

Entertainment and Education

Robot toys

Have you had a robot toy before? If you like robots, there's a strong chance you have - and there are certainly a lot of different robots to choose from. They can range in price from something you could buy with pocket money to something you'd probably have to save up for a few years to get. Over the next pages we will look through a few options on the market at the moment to give you an idea of the best robots around. Apologies if some of these items don't fit within your Christmas or birthday budget.

Most robot toys resemble either a humanoid or an animal and can have both entertainment as well as learning features. This duality of function (fun alongside education) carries through from robots from a preschool age to far older age groups too, obviously with increasing sophistication as well as price.

Playing back a pre-recorded voice over an internal speaker is a common feature of these types of robots and is likely triggered by some interaction by the user. The recorded voice can give the robot a strong character. Disney's animated robot WALL-E has been an inspiration to many robot toys that have appeared since the film. The other main feature of a robot's character is its eyes and they can tell the user a great deal about the mood the toy wishes to express (and if you have seen the toy Furby's eyes a whole lot more information besides that). Capacitive touch sensors that react to touch are great for interactive robot pets. Additional features common to these robots include touch, gesture and proximity recognition: if they use Passive Infrared (PIR) sensors that can detect body heat it can give the robot awareness of your presence.

Interactive pets

We could probably fill this book just with images of robot pets. Dogs, also known as 'man's best friend', are also the most popular robotic pet, though there are also robot cats, rabbits, seals and also imaginary animals. Furby is perhaps the most well-known animatronic toy and dates back to the 1990s. The part bird, part rodent-robot speaks its own language and grows in capability over time, developing its personality according to how people interact with it. In more recent versions there is also a mobile app to create further interaction and personalisation for

Furby. Probably the best robot dog of the many that exist is Sony's AIBO (Artificial Intelligence roBOt). First seen in 1999 this expensive, but much loved 'robodog' grows and develops from puppy-like behaviours when first switched on through play. Sony recently launched a new version, costing an eye-watering £2,000, which is more than the initial costs for most real dogs. As well as being full of clever tricks, the new AIBO can patrol your home like a guard dog. It has 4000 moving parts, motion detectors and cameras to realistically behave like a small dog, with the added benefits of not having holes bitten in your shoes or of having to clear up any dog poos!

Remotely controlled robots

A fairly common feature in toy robots is to be able to control their movement wirelessly. Radio-controlled vehicles are common place, and not expensive in themselves, typically using a hand-held joy pad or app joystick to enable vehicle movement. The key difference between what might be called a radio-controlled car and a controllable robot is probably just character – for example, having eyes and a voice.

One toy that is a great example of this is Boxer, shown here. It combines being able to move around on its own as well as by using its little controller. Though not as sophisticated as some of the upcoming toys, it demonstrates a great robot character with a small selection of interesting tricks and skills.

One company who, (before they went bust) did a great job of taking entertainment robotics to another level is Anki. Their robot Cozmo achieves a strong personality through a combination of movement of its robotic arm, animated eyes and robotic voice. This robot, though a tenth of the price of the Sony AIBO (under £200) was still a little too expensive for most people to afford. Cozmo uses the processing power of a connected mobile device to help power its artificial intelligence and the app also provides a range of activities and games. Like a little brother might, Cozmo reacts in amusing ways to both winning and losing games you play together.

Cozmo is able to recognise faces with its camera and links these with names you tell him, so he can greet people he sees. He can also explore the world under a user's directional control via a mobile app. Cozmo's camera allows you to see what he sees, which can be great for spying on siblings or parents or perhaps finding things you've lost under your bed!

FACT FILE

Animatronic is a word made from combining 'animate' with 'electronics'. Disney introduced the first animatronic characters in the film 'Mary Poppins' in 1964. Animatronics is mainly used to describe moving puppet characters, but most humanoid and animal robots also share the same electronic components. Servo motors, known as rotary or linear actuators provide joint and head movement to both.

Cozmo packs a lot of features into a package small enough to fit in your hand and is robustly built to handle being dropped or falling off a table. Another added benefit of Cozmo is that you can use Cozmo Code Lab (part of the mobile app) to programme your own activities for the little robot to perform.

These can be combinations of movement or animation, with facial and object recognition. Available at beginner and intermediate level, it's a good way to start to learn programming of robots and then push the boundaries of what your robot is capable of doing. This is the kind of functionality that is being given to an increasing number of robots aimed at owners who are eight or more years old.

Rolling and coding

A company who have also taken their direction toward learning and education is Sphero. As you might tell from the name, their robots have a particular shape ... they are spherical. The first enjoyment you will get from the product is just moving it around using the mobile-app. Sphero's technology was used to help power the toy version of the droid in the shape of an 8, BB-8 that first appeared in the Star Wars film The Force Awakens.

The company now make a range of predominantly spherical robots and their emphasis is on giving educational benefit as well as offering fun games to keep you occupied. More and more schools are seeing the benefits of using products like the Sphero Bolt (right) to give children an introduction to coding, perhaps you've been lucky enough to try one at school, if not at home? Bolt is only a little less expensive than the Anki Cozmo, but Sphero also has an entry level product (the Sphero mini, £50) that delivers most of the core movement experience of the Bolt. Both products use motor encoders, gyroscopes and accelerometers and work with the Edu app. The Edu app combines with Sphero products to give a great range of team and single user activities to progress your coding. The app allows beginners to draw simple paths for Sphero to follow, the next level allows users to build activities in blocks using the programming interface

Scratch and, finally, once you have the confidence, you can try to do this using the popular coding language JavaScript. It's no surprise these robots are starting to be seen in more and more classrooms around the world as the need for everyone to have at least basic computer coding skills becomes more apparent.

Battling bots

Fighting robots have regularly appeared on TV screens in the UK and US over the past twenty years in programmes like Robot Wars and BattleBots, where expert robot builders are pitted against each other and the 'house' (TV programme's own) robots in a squash-court sized battle arena to find a winner. These robots are actually dangerous to be close to as some wield hammers, axes and spikes, so the battles take place behind caged barriers. However, there are several safer options available, specifically for

battling robots, including a miniature version of the battle arena from the programme available from Hexbug.

Other options include a robot game that dates back to the 1960s that certainly isn't obviously dangerous called Rock 'Em Sock 'Em (see left) which has two robots in a boxing ring. Hand controllers move the robots and thumb buttons allow you to punch your opponent. The winner is the one who manages to make the other robot's head pop up. There are no electronics involved, so these toys are lacking sophistication to be identified as more than robot puppets.

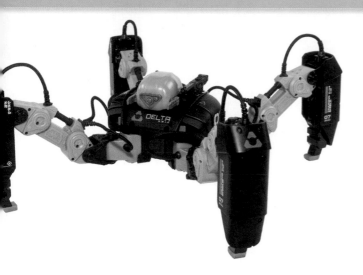

The other end of the spectrum for fighting bots is a robot called Super Anthony. These robots are used in public competitions against each other. They move using a Sony DS3 joypad and have a punching force of 45kg per servo, so are not really people or animal friendly.

One battling robot that takes things to another level but is much better suited to playing at home is the Mekamon robot from Reach Robotics. Mekamon was developed with the idea of having a mechanised Pokemon, a life-like character that lives across a mobile app with a physical robot version too. Mekamon is an advanced 4-legged robot that you control and battle with using a mobile phone or tablet. Not only can you battle one Mekamon versus another in the real world, but you can also battle your Mekamon versus others anywhere through the mobile app.

Your Mekamon is tracked using Augmented Reality (AR) on the screen in front of you, while your competitor is also tracked to move in the same space on the floor, so you can have a real, virtual battle. Mekamon have also released a ReachEdu app allowing a user to code their Mekamon to move, and it can also wave using one of its four robotic legs.

Building bots

If you are more of a builder than a battler, then there are plenty of options in this direction too. Rather than try to explain them all, we'll head straight to the best example of these kind of robots, which is Lego Mindstorms. As you probably already know, Lego sets are available from small, affordable gifts to huge scale kits and this is one of the latter ones. You do get a lot in the box, so most budding roboticists will definitely get value from the investment. These expensive toys target older children, but they can also be found in use the world over in schools and universities as a test bed for real world robotic ideas.

The strength of the product is the range of options it gives. As standard it has 3 servo motors (2 large, 1 medium sized), colour, touch and IR sensors. You can control your robot remotely via a supplied dedicated controller or use the Mindstorms app on a tablet or phone. The fact that you are using Lego, also means you can build your robot beyond the 5 suggested robots in the instructions, adding standard Lego bricks to make all kinds of 'walking, talking and thinking' robots. Owners of Lego Mindstorms kits have shared their ideas of what else to build online, these include a robot that can automatically solve a Rubik's Cube puzzle, taking it from a jumble of colours to the same colour on every side.

Social and Domestic Robots

The combination of social with domestic (also known as service or assistive) robots, could provide robot companions who are also capable helpers, making our lives more enjoyable and fulfilled. This kind of personal robot aims to be both a sophisticated machine that can autonomously complete manual chores as well as our robot personal assistant, nanny or butler, available to help organise us, educate us and perhaps even protect us and our children. Whether we ever achieve a single robot that can do our house work, such as cooking, cleaning and

ironing as well as being a robot personal organiser, is very difficult to envisage based on today's robots. The building blocks for this hybrid robot already exist with specific manual tasks such as vacuum cleaning being accomplished and, separately, voice assistants capable of understanding our natural language requests and responding with appropriate answers and responses.

For social robots to be successful, they need to be easy to interact with and the robots themselves need to be able to respond in a way we expect. A key aim within Human Robot Interactions (HRI) is to determine the social characteristics of humans that are effective when used by robots. Socially intelligent robots would be capable of natural interactions, which we discuss later in the book within the topic of artificial intelligence (AI).

> ❝ ...what we find is that people respond to robots a lot like they respond to people.
>
> *Cynthia Breazeal*
> *Social Robotics Pioneer* ❞

If you think about it, we are often trying to 'humanise' technology, that is, we treat it like a person or animal, known as anthropomorphising it. We call our cars by affectionate names, we say please and thank you when asking things of AI voice assistants, and we care about toys that are cute and desire attention. Because this is what our experience and learning as children has taught us to do with other humans, we extend these conventions to technology and even more so if the robots provide the same communication cues back to us.

Unlike robots, people behave randomly and don't stick to rules, so when robots collaborate with us there needs to be a lot of safety considerations for the robot not to be a danger to us. For this reason, social robots have proximity sensors to tell them when something, or someone is near, before they make contact with it. If we are working side-by-side, it is also important that robots communicate to us, not necessarily by speaking to us or alerting us, but by behaving in ways we understand. Most human communication is non-verbal (gestures and expressions), so robot communication needs to make best use of these unspoken cues. Some cues aren't even intended communication, for example, if your robot helper was picking up toys with you and you can see by its head and eye position which objects it was aiming to collect, this would help you avoid choosing the same item and bumping into each other.

Robot therapy

Robots that have a close relationship with humans have purposes other than being a personal assistant or helper. Of course, the previous section on toys showed plenty of robots that are fun to be around, but there are others that are more suited and targeted toward older people. The Paro (left) is a great example of a robot whose primary purpose is comfort and companionship for the elderly. Paro is extremely soft and cute to look at, it has 12 sensors under the fur that react to touch. When users stroke it, Paro reacts with soothing noises and motions, including moving its flippers. Another example of these kinds of robots is the Lovot, whose name comes from Love and Robot.

Robot helpers

One task that has found a suitable robot solution is vacuuming our floors. Due to their location and size, robot vacuum cleaners aren't a threat to our safety and with their onboard sensors and intelligence, they can generally keep themselves out of trouble too.

Usually working while you are out, one of these robot cleaners called Roomba builds a map of your house using its in-built camera, so it can autonomously clean your house. It avoids obstacles and knows not to fall down the stairs – it even knows when it needs to recharge, so it can keep cleaning through the day. The only thing that Roomba can't do is empty itself and take out the rubbish afterwards, but perhaps they are working on that too?

Humanoid helpers

There have been some terrific innovations in this area including Honda's Asimo and more recently Pepper and Nao from Softbank Robotics that all successfully perform a variety of functions in a humanoid form (see page 40 for more). They are effective communicators, and usually take roles in social environments as an alternative to a regular customer service personnel. They tend to be designed to be child sized so that they are more approachable. They can also be a great learning resource in educational settings, as they can interact with people effectively more than a computer and quickly help answer verbal questions given to them. Studies by a student

of Cynthia Breazeal found that robots help convey more empathy, engagement and collaboration compared to static communication tools, so there is a strong reason for us wanting to adopt them in the future. However, with the Softbank robots priced at £6,000 (Nao) and £20,000 (Pepper), they aren't affordable for everyday use just yet.

It may be interesting to ask yourself what your ideal robot companion would be like. Would it be an animal or person? What would it be able to do? Perhaps you can start with a list of all the things you'd rather not have to do, such as doing homework, presenting in class or sitting your exams? Though these may not be realistic, there are many things that robots might be able to do to help.

Bionics

An area of robotics that has fairly unique considerations, and perhaps the clearest benefits to humans, is bionics. Bionics involves robotic components that replace biological body parts and is already making a positive impact on people the world over. Anyone born without or having lost one or more of their arms or legs through disease or accidents, have typically used conventional prosthetics, but now have more natural movement and grip due to robotic innovations in bionics.

Bionic cochlear implants are also being used by people who cannot hear to regain that sense, by converting sound vibrations into information the brain can understand. When not substituting a missing or malfunctioning body part, bionics can also be used to enhance human body strength and performance by adding exo (external) skeletons. This might be for rehabilitation from injury, to combat a specific weakness or to allow people to do lifting and work beyond what their human body is capable of safely doing. As bionics have direct physical contact and can be worn, a great deal of thought has to be put into their design, in terms of functionality, for safety and also – when they are visible – in terms of the acceptance of the product by the intended user.

We talk about the uncanny valley in the section about robots designed to resemble humans in one way or another (p39). Studies have shown that robots and prosthetics that try but fall short of being a convincing replica of a human or a body part, can be very unappealing – we see them as either creepy or scary – and we wouldn't choose to be near them. Open Bionics research found that their users didn't want a robotic replacement to attempt to look like a real arm. They wanted something better.

Bionic arms

Prosthetics were invented thousands of years ago to help replace missing body parts, in fact they didn't change significantly until recently. People alive today who were born with one arm might have been offered a hook as a substitute for a hand. Fortunately, some bright people wanted to challenge the kinds of prosthetic solutions made available to people with limb differences the world over. A good example is the Bristol based robotics laboratory Open Bionics who have created a unique and open-sourced method (i.e. they share aspects of their work openly to others) of achieving appealing robotic arm prosthetics. They make their multi-grip bionic 'Hero Arms' available for less cost and a lot less time than other robotic prosthetics by using the relatively new techniques of 3D scanning and 3D printing.

Tilly Lockey

Also, due to a licensing agreement with Disney, their arms are created around characters in Disney and Star Wars films to make them very desirable to have. They focus on the needs of children aged 8 and over (and if they are lucky enough adults can have them too). As the company says, they turn disabilities into superpowers and the people who use their arms feel this positive change too. Where they may have felt stigmatised due to an unattractive prosthetic previously, being able to add a functioning bionic arm and especially one branded with characters from films, gives them a positive talking point and a sense of pride around their uniqueness.

3D Scanning and 3D printing

These two technologies are enabling companies like Open Bionics to drastically reduce the complication and cost in providing bionic limbs. Previously, doctors and clinicians would take a plaster cast in order to build a made-to-measure socket to fit with the existing part of the limb. The whole process could take 3 months. For a growing child, this length of time would mean that the arm would likely not fit by the time it was ready to use. 3D scanners attach to mobile phones and it only takes a minute to get the 360-degree pictures needed to accurately measure an amputated arm. Low cost 3D printers are fed with plastic filament (a bit like a long, coiled plastic wire) and build up a design, one layer after another to make plastic products from computer designs. The main drawback of using 3D printing is that it takes a long time to produce individual items. However, when you are making unique parts for each customer in different colours and materials as Open Bionics do, 3D printing is the best possible solution for manufacturing. Within a week of taking the 3D scan, Open Bionics can deliver a completely finished light-weight robotic arm ready for use. Hero Arms are used for lower arm amputees and can be pushed onto the existing limb to allow users to manipulate the thumb and fingers in various grips. The whole process and ultimately the product that the user has is a massive improvement over the prosthetic arms previously available to them. As technology advances, it's easy to see how traditional medicine is being pushed to one side with patients gaining clearer benefits as well as time and cost savings all round.

Bionic technology

Recreating the dexterity in a human hand is extremely difficult; there are 27 individual bones and over 30 muscles working together in a highly complex way. Open Bionics' Hero Arms make use of electromyography (EMG) sensors to enable specific muscle movements in the user's arm to be translated to allow the coordinated movement of the Hero Arm's fingers and thumb. Mechanomyography (MMG) sensors are also used in bionic applications. As opposed to EMG that looks for electrical signals in muscles, MMG uses the mechanical, physical movement in the muscle as the trigger for bionic movement.

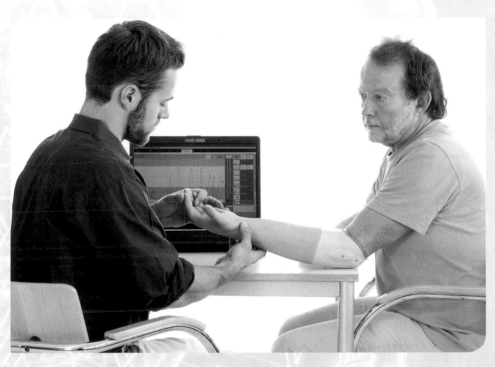

Bionic legs

Legs and feet also have complex muscle movement to allow you to balance and walk, of course we also enjoy the chance to jump, run, climb and dance which only add to the complexity of movement, strength and control needed. Simple fixed prosthetic legs, even when light weight, can be very uncomfortable for leg amputees to use due to the soreness when fitting to the existing leg (the socket) and the lack of fluidity of movement in the false leg that causes back and other body pain. One person who sought to change this is a US mountain climber Hugh Herr, who lost both of his legs to frostbite in a mountaineering expedition aged 17. Rather than put Dr Herr off the idea of climbing, it made him more determined to climb and create better ways to use his lower limbs with prosthetic climbing attachments. His inventions and academic achievements literally moved him and other amputees in ways that wouldn't have been possible otherwise.

Herr continued to focus on methods of enhancing life for those with amputated legs and his company created a unique foot-angle bionic limb system called the Empower Ankle. The robotic ankle system helps provide mechanically aided walking for hundreds of amputees including veterans of war who have had their legs amputated due to mines and other improvised explosive devices.

> " *A great narrative of this century is humanity building the fundamental science and technology to eliminate disability*
>
> Dr Hugh Herr "

Connected Autonomous Vehicles

Cars, like all other technology around us, are rapidly becoming more connected to the internet and their capabilities are becoming more 'intelligent'. This means probably in about 20 years' time we are likely to be able to buy extremely reliable self-driving or 'robot' cars as standard. This is pretty amazing, when you think that around twenty years ago, it was still fairly common for people to use maps and rely on sign posts to know how to get to where they were headed. In-car navigation and especially Global Positioning System (GPS) navigation, better known as satellite navigation or satnav systems were only introduced to commercial vehicles in 1990.

Society of Automotive Engineers (SAE) Automation Levels

0: Vehicles have no automation

1: Driver assistance, support but no control

2: Partly automated, mainly driver controlled, but some automation

3: Highly automated, in some situations the driver can disengage e.g., motorway driving

5: Full automation, no-one can drive, people on board are passengers only

4: Fully automated driving, the vehicle is self-driving, but has a driver who can e.g., sleep on the journey

During the 1990s portable satnav systems were bought and attached to car windscreens to provide 'turn-by-turn' navigation for the many ca[ ]hat didn't have it fitted as standard. These days you can find these same navigation features on most smartphones you can buy. The technology in cars has improved so much now that useful information and graphics can be projected on the windscreen in front of the driver using heads up displays (HUDs).

Alongside satnav, other drivers' aids have become much more sophisticated. Car manufacturers have added cameras and sensors to aid drivers with various aspects of the driving experience including parking, being aware of another vehicle's proximity and also to stay in a single lane while driving. Not only are cars now providing better visual and audio alerts to the driver, but also robotic control of the brakes and steering wheel to help prevent collisions, as well as parking at the push of a button. If you look at the diagram (left) you can see we are currently at the second to third level in the evolution of cars driving autonomously (i.e. no human driver). Some current vehicles achieve level 3, but it is unclear if this is with favourable conditions i.e., good weather and 'predictability' of the driving environment.

Collision avoidance systems

Safety is the most important feature of an autonomous car and one aspect of keeping people safe is avoiding vehicles ever coming into contact with other road users. Accidents caused by cars and other road vehicles are responsible for killing people every day across the world, so the need for this solution is not purely to achieve a driverless car, it will help us avoid needless loss of life. It is definitely not as simple as it sounds and this is because driving is a great human skill. We are very good at using our brains to judge whether a situation is safe or not and to react to it, within a fraction of a second. Any system that needs to react to driving situations and hazards has to be extremely fast and extremely aware of everything around it to make the right decisions.

To do this, collision avoidance systems use either all-weather radar or LIDAR combined with cameras that provide image recognition into the system. The systems take action when the vehicle is travelling at lower speeds (50kmh /31mph) by applying brakes, but at higher speeds controlling the steering is more appropriate, assuming there is space to move, for example into another lane. The braking side of this system is called autonomous emergency braking (AEB) and is now implemented as standard in the majority of vehicles (over 80% in 2019) made for the US market by Tesla, Mercedes-Benz, Volvo, Toyota/Lexus, BMW and Audi.

However, controlling brakes and steering due to other vehicles and hazards proximity, should not make us feel we have autonomous driving nearly solved. When you next take a journey either by car or by bike on a road, try to think of all the decisions you are making every step of the way. Where am I going? How fast? Whose turn is it on the roundabout? Will that dog run into the road? Is that driver letting me out? That is a good question for the autonomous car. Will it be 'polite' if a car needs to be let out of a junction if doing so is safe and will make little difference to its journey time? Let's hope so. Did the car also spot the cyclist racing down the hill, while it was being polite and letting you into the road? Hopefully you can see the complexity. It is especially complex when you add thousands of these cars and all other road users making similar decisions in the same city space, all needing connectivity to the internet and processing millions of decisions throughout their journey. These are part of vehicle to everything (V2X) systems and it is still being decided whether these should use either WLAN (like Wi-Fi used in the home) or 5G cellular (like mobile phones are starting to use).

Experts believe we are still decades away from freely using autonomous cars in public environments. There has to be a reliably high bandwidth data network for all the information to be shared – as it happens – and also a 'smart city' environment full of sensors, signage and transmitters to enable it to work, which will take a lot of time and money. There are also concerns about cars being hacked by other people and about how to get home if a sensor goes wrong.

To get around many of these issues, there are some 'driverless' robot cars and lorries that use remote operators to keep the passengers and other road users safe. The remote operators are experienced drivers with screens around them to observe the whole vehicle's view in real time. They have control over the car, using a steering wheel and pedals – like driving game accessories - to take over from the vehicle if they think the situation needs it. The reaction time to respond to any situation will be the driver's normal reaction time, plus the time it takes to send the live video of the car and then the time for the action made to be sent to the robot vehicle and acted upon there. Only the fastest most reliable wireless systems will allow this, and extra space will be needed around these vehicles to give them more time to react and stop. What do you think about seeing a car with no driver overtaking your car on the motorway?

Industrial Robots

Although we've seen many different applications for robots in the book so far, the most popular uses for robotics today are covered in this section.

To better understand the various types of robots, Japan Robot Association's (JARA) created these classifications:

Class	Type	Description
1	**Manual handling device**	These robots have multiple degrees of freedom, but all of their actions are performed under the direct control of an operator.
2	**Fixed sequence robot**	These robots repeat a fixed sequence of actions without needing to be controlled by an operator. However, the sequence of actions they perform cannot be modified (i.e. they are not programmable).
3	**Variable sequence robot**	Similar to class 2, except that the sequence of actions can be reprogrammed easily allowing it to be quickly adapted to perform new tasks.
4	**Playback robot**	This type of robot is first guided through a sequence of actions by an operator, then repeats the same actions automatically.
5	**Numerical control robot**	This type of robot moves through a sequence of actions, which it receives in the form of numerical data.
6	**Intelligent robot**	A robot that senses its environment and responds to changes in it in order to continue performing its function.

The Robotics institution of America (RIA) doesn't include class 1 or 2 in their list of robot types. We have included some Manual Handling Devices here but agree that a Fixed Sequence Robot (one that can't be programmed) isn't a great robot.

Japan is the world's leading manufacturer of industrial robots with a number of large robotic companies, including world leader Fanuc who have installed over half a million robots worldwide. Many of these robots are used in the car industry (particularly in the US and Germany). The next most popular use is for electronics/electrical assembly (predominantly in Singapore and Asia) and the metal and machinery industry is the next biggest use. South Korea has the most robots per human workers in the world with over six hundred robot workers for every ten thousand human employees.

Robots help us achieve work objectives that we'd struggle to do on our own. They are really useful when things are either too dangerous or dirty for us to do, and they're also fantastic for doing things precisely, which we might struggle to do ourselves. Accuracy and repeatability are both critical in manufacturing where high quality is paramount. The two words mean slightly different things, accuracy means it can achieve a position as close as possible to the desired value. Repeatability means it can achieve the same position again and again. In robotics repeatability is the more important measure and equates to precision. These 3 bullseye images help explain this difference.

Accurate, but not repeatable

Repeatable, but not accurate

Repeatable and accurate

Another key performance parameter for industrial robots is payload, which is essentially how much weight the robot can lift. This weight is measured as the tool attached to the wrist plus the object it is lifting up (see diagram opposite), which is why many tools are made of a lightweight material, like aluminium with hollow insides, so as not to weigh too much. Useful payloads start from around 5kg, Fanuc's strongest robot can handle 2300kg.

Robot arms

The first industrial robot made by George Devol called Unimate, was a robot arm. These arms were used in large factories by car manufacturers for loading, welding and spraying. These continue to be among the most popular applications and tasks for robots today. Many other industrial uses for robots have also become significant, including mobile robots for pick-and-place and palletising, for example to help you receive goods you order online. Robot arms – also known as manipulators - continue to be the predominant form factor (shape and style) of robots in industry as they are ideal for achieving wide ranging, controlled movement.

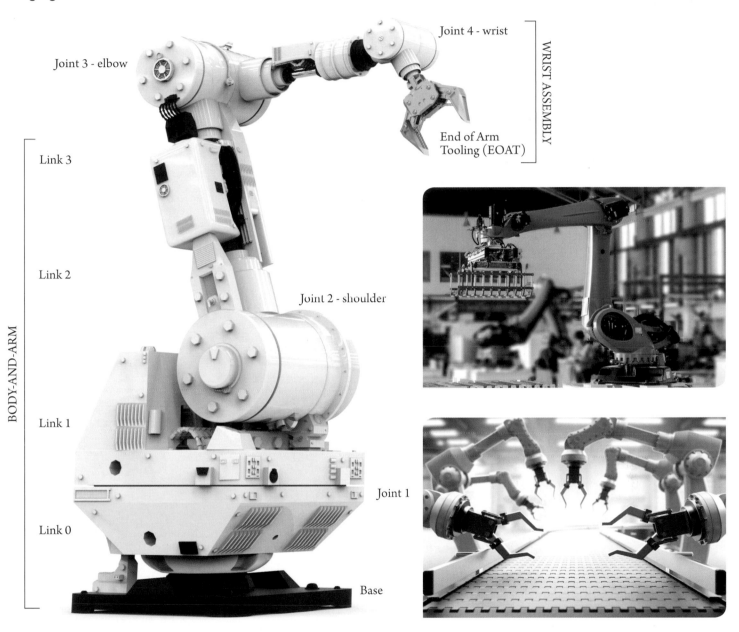

This robot arm is an articulated manipulator. These are the most popular arms and work in a similar way to a human arm. They consist of two main sections, the body-and-arm and the wrist (or flange) assembly. They have at least 2 revolute (circular) joints that move together to position the end of arm tool (EOAT) or end effector, in the right place to do the intended job. The EOAT can travel on a specific path or in a variety of motions, for example to avoid obstacles and complete multiple tasks including changing the tool during the cycle of the programme (or sequence) to perform different jobs on the same object.

The area that a robot needs to move freely in is called its work envelope or work space. Often this area is a lot larger than the equivalent area a human would need to do the job as robot arms don't typically work as well in confined spaces as we do. In many cases robots will be caged within their work envelope to ensure no humans can come to harm; however, as we find more uses for robots, they are more often needed to be working side-by-side with humans. We'll look at this in a few pages time; these robots are called cobots (short for collaborative robots).

Robot reference frames

A range of reference frames provide the robot programmer with different ways of viewing and controlling how the robot arm behaves. The different approaches fix specific locations about the robot manipulator; the robot's environment, its base, its joint or its tool. In the world reference frame, the x-y-z axes plot all the movement of the robot arm relative to a fixed location in the robot's environment. All movement will be measured parallel to these fixed axes, no robot arm or tool movement will change their orientation. The image shows the base of the robot for the world reference frame, which is a common starting point for this approach.

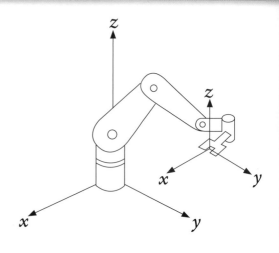

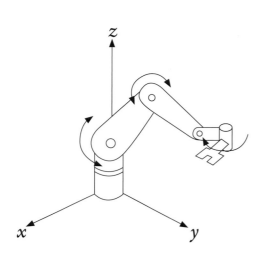

The joint reference frame uses every individual joint as a reference toward overall movement. Only one joint is considered for movement at a time. Robot arms are either revolute (circular/rotary) or prismatic (straight line/linear). The image shows revolute joints where co-ordinates are angles, for linear joints these can be pulses or encoder counts.

A tool reference frame specifies the movements of the robot's tool relative to the x-y-z axes in a cartesian frame. Cartesian is another name for the x-y-z axes as shown in the diagram (right) that go in entirely different directions or 'planes'. The centre for the cartesian axes can be the end of the tool mounting plate at the point where the tool attaches, or the tip of e.g., a welding gun tool or it may even be the middle of e.g., a gripping tool.

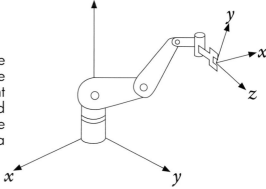

Control methods

The control methods for servo controlled programmable robots are point-to-point or continuous path. Point to point is (as you can imagine) using specific locations or points, that are stored by or provided to the robot. The robot is then given a reference frame as a preferred way to move through the points. The user can control the speed of the arm, this method tends to be used with pick-and-place and loading tasks. The alternative, continuous path, needs to store a lot more information as it tracks where all the joints and the end effector are positioned. This method is needed for close control in spraying and welding applications.

Degrees of freedom

The number of joints in the robot's body, arm and wrist, give its movement a number of degrees of freedom: that is the number of independent directions it can move its tool within a programmed sequence. A robotic joint is equal to one degree of freedom and typically you have a minimum of six: 3 for position (left-right, forward-backward, and up-down) relating to the body and arm, and 3 for orientation (yaw, pitch and roll) in the wrist.

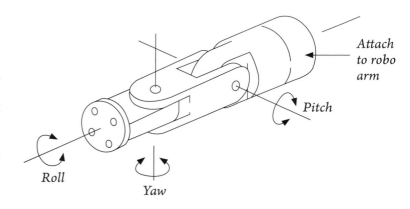

Kinematics

Articulated manipulators (see page 26) are just one class of kinematic configuration in industrial robotics. Kinematics means the arrangement of rigid members and joint which determine the robot's movement.

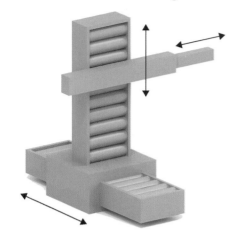

Cartesian Robot

These types of robots are made of 3 linear (or prismatic) joints, meaning they only move in straight lines. The work envelope they occupy is rectangular and is often enclosed in a box. Cartesian is the most common 3D printer configuration and is also often used in computer (CNC) lathes. Also called gantry robots, these machines can be used for chart plotting, milling or drilling materials in a production line or can be large in size and used to 'pick and place'.

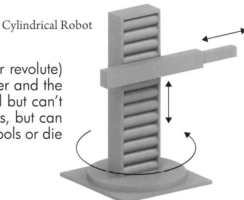

Cylindrical Robot

Cylindrical coordinate robots combine two linear joints with a circular (or revolute) one, the up-and-down motion is typically provided by a pneumatic cylinder and the rotation provided by motors and gears. Their work envelope is cylindrical but can't quite reach through 360 degrees. They are not commonly used these days, but can be used for assembly operations, spot welding and handling at machine tools or die casting machines.

Spherical Robot

Spherical or Polar robots have three (or more) axes of movement, the ring shape of their work envelope is due to having two rotary joints and one linear. Like the cylindrical robot, spherical robots typically have a circular joint on their base and a linear extending joint on their arm, the difference is their wrist can also rotate. Spherical robots are used in many similar applications to cylindrical ones but are additionally used for arc and gas welding.

Selective Compliance Assembly Robot Arms (SCARA) make use of two parallel revolute joints to help them be a fast-moving robot highly suited to assembly, as well as pick and place work, applying sealant and handling machine tools. The linear (prismatic) joint allows the height of the operating arm to be adjusted.

SCARA Robot

Parallel Robot

Parallel configuration or Delta robots are ideal for pick and place, light assembly and packaging activities. They are also the basis for movement in flight simulators. Their advantage is being able to move at high speed. They have linear joints positioned at angles to move a platform (where an end of arm tool can be fitted) in very accurate positions, although within a fairly confined cone-shaped work envelope.

End of arm tools (EOAT)

Whichever the choice of manipulator, the body-and-arm section works with the wrist to give the tool the ability to move reliably, accurately and repeatably to perform a function or task. When programmed correctly these tasks can be done relentlessly without sleep, toilet breaks or refreshment and performed to a consistently high level of quality.

The jobs robot arms do are principally making, packing, sorting or moving. The ability to perform a task has a lot to do with the choice of kinematic configuration and the strength or payload of the robot, but the correct choice of end of arm tool (EOAT also called end effector) is critical. As we show here, there are numerous EOAT options to choose between, fortunately many robots are able to change tools during a cycle, widening their potential use across a number of activities.

Alongside the purpose of the robot, other factors that need consideration when choosing tools include the size and shape of the part you are working on or moving, its weight (which makes up the payload when combined with the tool weight) and its surface type and rigidity. Beyond this you'll need to understand your required speed of action or cycle time, how precise the work needs to be and any specific limitations or needs within the environment the robot is working in.

Grippers

Typical grippers have 2 or more pliers or fingers to grip and can even resemble a hand when this best suits the application. A key difference between these grippers apart from fingers is the servo or actuator mechanism that allows them to operate, which can be pneumatic (compressed air), hydraulic (compressed fluid, typically oil) or electric. There are various advantages of one system over another and other factors, for example the possibility of having oil leaks that forbid hydraulic systems being used in food and pharmaceutical industries. These industries often use grippers that, rather than using a thumb and forefinger grip, use suction (vacuum) cups to pick and pack items, for example fruit, that may otherwise be bruised, marked or crushed due to their delicate skin and irregular shape.

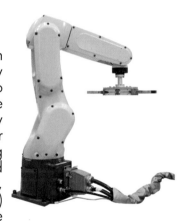

Welding torches

The car industry was an important early adopter of robot arms and this is one of the industries that would make use of welding in one of its many forms, including Arc, MIG, Laser and Electron Beam. The wrist and tool can also have a wire feed to allow the robot to have more control of the process.

In truth, pretty much any device or accessory can be mounted at the end of a robot arm if there is a use for it, including tools for paint spraying, cutting, sanding, drilling, water spraying, cleaning, gluing and polishing. Other features of end of arm tools are sensors to avoid collisions and also attachments that can help the robot switch between one tool and another. These tool changers or couplers typically use pneumatic (air) pressure and lock a tool together with a master automatically, passing through utilities such as electric signals or pneumatic pressure to help the tool operate.

Programming industrial robots

A company that is thinking about buying a robot arm to help speed up and improve its processes, needs to be able to weigh up the costs. A robot arm itself typically costs tens of thousands of pounds, but that's not all, you also need to think about installation, training and programming. Programming is the method of instructing the robot to perform the desired movements and actions in operation without human intervention. Ideally programming should be fairly easy to understand and follow, so that you don't need an expert software programmer to rewrite

the robot programme or change it at any point. As introducing a robot into a workplace is expensive, the main way the costs will be justified is if you think of using that robot for several years and see the savings over this time. It is also very useful if you have robots that are capable of being programmed to achieve a number of different operations as was originally envisaged.

George Devol, the inventor of the first industrial robot, had the idea after seeing a lot of different tooling machines become redundant as their specific need was outdated. He called his invention the 'Programmed Article Transfer', before becoming commercialised as 'The Unimate Industrial Robot' with help from Joe Engelberger, who was a keen reader of Isaac Asimov (who coined the term 'robotics'). The idea was that these new robotic arms didn't need to be specialised for any particular task, they could adapt by using different tools and programming for the new task.

The Unimate robot was controlled using a simple teaching programme, most like the playback robot from the table on p25. The robot was moved manually (by hand), and the coordinates of the position of the joints were stored. After several positions had been stored the robot was able to go through the position of the joints in a sequence. In the 1950s computers and programming were only just starting to emerge from room-sized monstrosities toward the desktop computers and laptops we know today. Unimate was state-of-the-art at this time.

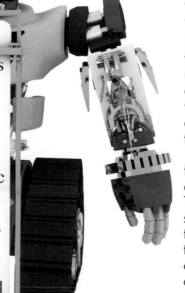

In 1977, to improve its product range, Unimation acquired (bought) Vicarm, who had an advanced programming language called VAL (Variable Assembly Languages) for their PUMA robot arms. The combination was strong and a great asset to the Unimation company. VAL allowed robot operators to do both online and offline programming thought the use of the growing category of computers, so programming was not limited to leading the robot through its operation, you could code offline with a language that was both easy to understand as well as use.

You may be interested to learn that Unimation Inc. weren't able to defend their once strong market leading position (monopoly) in robotics in the 1960s and early 1970s. They became uncompetitive when Japanese and German manufacturers developed better quality alternatives to Unimation's range. Also, by the mid 1970s when the industry moved away from hydraulic driven mechanisms toward electric ones, Unimation were slow to react. They lost their prized GM account (and significant sales) to Fanuc who went on to lead the robotics market themselves, as they do today. VAL3 is still in use with the company that went on to buy the Unimation company's assets, called Stäubli.

FACT FILE

Three kinds of robotic drive systems are generally used, they are:
1) Electric, now the most popular and widely available drive system. Uses electric motors and servos to actuate (move) individual joints
2) Hydraulic, the first form of robotic manipulator, uses hydraulic pistons and rotary vane actuators. Still in use for heavy lifting and high-power applications
3) Air, compressed air pistons provide the actuation and drive, ideal for smaller robots and transfer (pick-and-place) applications

Robot programming – entry methods

The two key methods that robotic appliances are programmed for are online and offline. Online methods are physically close to the robot and so-named as the robot is switched 'on', like a control panel. Offline entry means not having to be connected to the robot or for it to be on, the robot is programmed by a separate computer which could be anywhere. Offline programming has benefitted in recent years by the entire operation being graphically mapped and simulated. Many robots have both online and offline functionality available, and there are useful benefits with and reasons you'd want to use both.

Online programming

Why used? Easy to use and understand, can be operated by unskilled workers (ones that aren't computer programmers) and gives immediate access to change operation.

• **Teach pendant** – a handheld tablet-like screen used to control the movement and speed of a robot arm, with at least one physical button for an emergency stop either on the front or on the back called a 'deadman switch'.

• **Lead through programming** – the robot arm is moved in the motion it is intended to take in the work cycle, the robot's linked computing capability stores the path, so it can be replayed whenever needed. Manual lead through is pretty much as described for the first Unimate robot arms, whereas powered lead through uses a teach pendant for movement.

Offline programming

Why used? Working with a computer allows complex calculations and operations to be quickly computed and therefore improves accuracy. Once written, a programme can be shared with many robots quickly and changes to the programme can be made offline, without stopping the operation of the robot until the new programme is ready.

Virtual environment programming/CAD and CAM systems - Can make use of very user-friendly environments including visual simulations of workstations, robots and tools to accurately and safely replicate operation, before being put into use.

Robot programming languages

Unlike desktop computing, which benefited from a small number of operating systems for software developers to focus on and for wide ranging programmes to thrive, industrial robotics manufacturers have each developed their own proprietary programming languages and environments. This means there are as many programming languages as there are robot manufacturers.

This makes it tough for anyone to be an expert across all robot languages. It also means that robotic languages have stayed a little behind the curve of what other computers are capable of doing, meaning they are less advanced than

Industrial Robot brand	Language name
ABB	RAPID
Comau	PDL2
Fanuc	Karel
Kawasaki	AS
Kuka	KRL
Stäubli	VAL3
Yaskawa	INFORM
Universal Robots	URScript

other technology areas as a result. An open source operating system for robots, ROS-Industrial hopes to give a platform for future programming to become more advanced and open to all and seems to be gaining wider acceptance.

Robots working side-by-side with us

Collaborative robots, also known as co-robots or cobots, are robots that are designed to work side-by-side with humans within a collaborative workspace. The idea of cobots is to help humans be more efficient and effective, substituting us when the robot can either do the job better or is preferred to do the job, meaning the human would be free to do something (for example) less repetitive or dangerous. The key requirement of a cobot is to be absolutely safe around humans, it has to 'expect the unexpected' in terms of human behaviour and be able to react to ensure we aren't hurt by it in any way.

Cobots aim to be an extra pair of hands for a worker, some designs of cobots are literally trying to add a pair of hands to a human body. More usually they take the form of a robotic arm or 2 arms as shown in the image (right).

The main problem with providing safe robots is that they are less likely to have the power (or payload) of robots that do not have these concerns. However, with better intelligence and control, through onboard and external sensors, cobot arms have been created that can lift more than 20kg next to a human. If the robot arm comes into contact with anything it stops automatically, so no shield or cage is needed.

Cobots were invented around twenty years ago to simply be a robot arm people could work next to. As we've learnt, robots can be any shape and size and there are many other types of robot that could be a huge help in the work place, if they were able to be working closely with us.

Mobile robots

One huge area for human collaboration with robots is within online retailers. Some of Amazon's fulfilment centres are enormous in scale; think about a football pitch, going from one end to the other, then do that 20 times – that's how long some of these warehouses are. Then again, if you think about it, you can pretty much order anything from Amazon and have it delivered the next day, so understandably they need to carry a lot of stock and be able to deliver that to you quickly and efficiently.

The main aim of Amazon's mobile robotic fulfilment systems is to help human workers focus on their packing roles without having to walk around the warehouse to get what they need. The robots are automated guided vehicles (AGVs) that slide underneath, lift and then carry portable storage units full of products intelligently around the factory floor to the stations that the workers are operating in. Amazon have installed over 45,000 of these robots in their facilities so far.

These AGV robots are guided by a barcode system on the floor and can lift over 1300Kg on pallets. They know to recharge their batteries themselves for 5 minutes every hour to keep going throughout the day. These aren't the only robots Amazon are working with. CEO Jeff Bezos has stated Amazon will be delivering products to people's homes using drones (like the one in this image) in the very near future.

Robotic Farming

Farming is an industry ripe (pardon the pun) for transformation through the use of robotics. 'Agritech' describes the use of technology to make farming more efficient, and food growing processes more effective. Interestingly, if you look back in history, at the very start of the 18th century in the UK, various forms of agricultural technology innovations including the plough and the seed drill, alongside ideas such as crop rotation, helped vastly improve the yield of crops and lead the country towards better nutrition and a rise in the population. This was the precursor to the industrial revolution, now known as the first industrial revolution (between 1760 and 1840). We are currently in the fourth industrial revolution where robotics, automation and AI are some of the key technologies enabling great improvements in a wide range of industries and aspects of life.

If you were an owner of a large field in the past 20 years and wanted to grow a crop there, the principles haven't changed significantly since the first industrial revolution, although machinery has advanced with tractors, combine harvesters and the like. Robotics, AI and automation are now being introduced to help in a number of ways, from sowing seeds to nurturing them through growth, weeding and of course harvesting them at the end, even packing them for distribution to shops. Robots don't just give better crop yields, the benefits are also in reducing energy and water consumption and the use of herbicides and pesticides, which in turn also has a positive effect on the environment as wildlife is not killed unnecessarily.

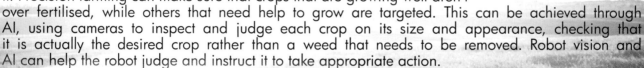

Smaller robots doing these jobs also mean tractors are used less, reducing the compacting of soil (from the weight of the tractor) which can make those areas less productive for crops. Compacted soil has a negative environmental effect as it increases waterlogging and destroys soil fauna and earthworms, who do a great job to irrigate the soil by moving through it. Precision farming can make sure that crops that are growing well aren't over fertilised, while others that need help to grow are targeted. This can be achieved through AI, using cameras to inspect and judge each crop on its size and appearance, checking that it is actually the desired crop rather than a weed that needs to be removed. Robot vision and AI can help the robot judge and instruct it to take appropriate action.

The amount of money required to automate a process using robotics can be very substantial for any industry and certainly costs are a big consideration for farmers, when margins on farm produce can be fairly slight. Costs for moving to new robotic methods can include equipment, installation, programming and training. To justify the investment, it is likely that the robotic system will need to remain in use for quite some time, but with robotics being so new and an unknown quantity for most, it is difficult for farmers to take the risks of investing so much money. The Small Robot Company has a great answer for this, it offer farming as a service (FaaS) charged on a per hectare subscription fee and delivered using a team of robots (Tom, Dick and Harry). The three robots each provide a distinct function and operate with centralised computing from Wilma, its artificial intelligence (AI) 'digital farm' containing a growing knowledge base of locations, soils and crops.

Robots in Space

Using robots to help us explore space makes complete sense. There are numerous advantages of robots over humans for space exploration, importantly robots are easier to manage as they don't need rest or food and don't create waste, like we do. Safety is the first consideration in space travel and the main reason that robots are preferable to humans; ideally, there shouldn't be any risk to life. Most aspects of space travel and planet exploration are dangerous, certainly take-off and landing, but every step of the journey relies on complex planning and attention to detail.

Here are the biggest hazards for humans according to NASA, the US based National Aeronautics and Space Administration:

- **Space radiation** – in space the sun's rays are very dangerous to us and difficult to protect against

- **Distance from Earth** – the time to reach even the nearest planets is measured in months

- **Isolation and confinement** – that's a lot of time waiting to arrive, and more time means more risk

- **Lack of gravity** – has an effect on our bones, muscles and blood pressure

- **Hostile environments** – Earth, even at the North Pole, never gets as extreme as some other planets

Probably the most inhospitable place to land in our solar system (besides the Sun) is Venus. Though a similar sized planet to Earth, and one of the nearest to us, no known life on earth could possibly survive there. The temperature of the Venusian surface is 465 degrees Celsius (enough to melt lead), its atmosphere is 96.5% carbon dioxide (toxic to us) and with a pressure equivalent to 89 Earth atmospheres, we'd also be squashed like a grape. You'd be frankly mad to volunteer to go on a trip to Venus, sending a robot would be a much better option. As yet, no robots have actually ventured to Venus, only remotely controlled probes have landed on the surface and survived long enough to use their mineral-testing sensors, cameras and transmitters before failing and going silent. Robots (often with remote control, but with increasing autonomy) have been numerous times to the moon (these robots are essentially 'probes on wheels' called rovers) and a key destination planet has been Mars.

Mars Rovers

There are many reasons why we want to reach other planets, we are seeking to understand if other life forms exist, if they did they exist or if they could ever exist on these planets, we also want to know what these planets are made of and what their history in the universe was. The advantage of a rover over a probe is the ability to move around and take samples in a wide area rather than just the location of its landing. The first Mars Rover landed over 20 years ago in 1997, there have been further rover missions approximately every eight years, each larger, more sophisticated and more ambitious than its predecessor. Each has helped give us more understanding of Mars; its current state and how it evolved over billions of years.

The most recent rover to visit Mars was sent by NASA in 2012 and called Curiosity. It cost $2.5 billion dollars to take this six-wheeled car-sized robot to Mars. It was a moving science lab with 17 cameras, various tools including a drill, spectrometers, radiation detectors, environmental sensors and atmospheric sensors to leave no stone unturned.

The previous missions had suggested water existed on Mars, but Curiosity proved that 4 billion years ago the planet was a water world; what has become known as the red planet was once a largely blue one with salt water seas. Future robot missions to Mars aim to examine if we will be able to live on and colonise Mars in the future.

Remote Controlled Vehicles

Some official robotic classifications don't consider devices that are only able to operate through the direct control of humans to be 'real' robots. Though remote-controlled vehicles may not be autonomous, they do share most of the features of the robots we've already discussed in the book, so we think they deserve to be mentioned. These kinds of robots undertake some of the most hazardous activities; doing things we'd rather not risk doing ourselves or perhaps couldn't do on our own. Many space exploring robots have been remotely controlled, but there are other hazardous environments for people to be exposed to.

Bomb disposal

A man-made problem very grateful for a robotic solution is bomb disposal. This military activity aims to defuse or in some other way safeguard live explosive devices. Explosives were originally designed to destroy objects, such as bridges and buildings or military vehicles such as tanks, but of course they also have the potential to kill and seriously injure people. Due to this potential threat to life it takes the bravest of people to approach an explosive device and try to make it safe. The requirement to have effective bomb disposal methods grew in significance through the First World War and into the Second World War, especially when bombs with unknown fuse lengths were dropped on civilian populations, like the Blitz bombing of London. The terrorist bombing activities of the IRA in Northern Ireland and England claimed the lives of 23 British bomb disposal specialists between 1969 and 1997, before peace was achieved between the opposing sides. During this conflict the first robot for bomb disposal called the wheelbarrow (1972) was designed. This tank-tracked machine aimed to save the lives of bomb disposal experts it has gone on to safeguard many hundreds of lives. It works by getting close enough to the explosive device to squirt a jet of water onto the bomb and disable its electronic circuitry.

Bomb disposal robots have become more advanced as robotic technology and wireless technology has improved. The need has also become greater in places of conflict due to the increased use of improvised explosive devices (IEDs) as a method of attack. Bomb disposal robots are now equipped with high-spec cameras which can see in all directions as well as in total darkness. They use a manoeuvrable arm, similar to an industrial robotic arm, with a key feature of being easily removed and swapped with a replacement if damaged. Another recent innovation is that the end of arm tools can have haptic feedback, allowing the operator to feel the object they are disarming.

Nuclear waste disposal

Cleaning up nuclear waste has become a focus for robotic technology since the Three Mile Island nuclear disaster in 1979 and it was also used after the Chernobyl disaster in 1986. As is true of radiation in space, radiation from nuclear materials is very harmful to us and can cause death. Hazmat or decontamination suits are the protective clothing we use to stay safe when near radiation but take a long time to put on and are only effective for 2 hours. Robots offer a far safer and longer duration of use for work in nuclear power stations or to help after a nuclear accident or disaster. These robots can also be fitted with all kinds of sensors and cameras to help detect radiation and any other possible threats to human life, with their operators far enough away from the robot not to have any concern for their safety.

Subsea Robotics

AUVs and ROVs

If you want to explore the oceans without getting wet, or even going underwater, you can either use autonomous underwater vehicles (UAVs) or remotely operated underwater vehicles (known by the abbreviated acronym, ROV). ROVs were first conceived for military uses in the 1950s and began with the purpose of locating and recovering practise mines and torpedoes for the Royal Navy. They are agile and easy to control robots that are connected via a cable (tethered) to a ship or floating structure to allow information to be sent and received. The length of that cable (as well as the strength under pressure of the ROV itself) gives them an effective operating depth to a maximum of 6000 metres. UAVs are robot submarines with neither a pilot nor a tether and can also go to depths of 6000 metres travelling without guidance for several days at a time.

To help get a sense of these depths, the deepest anyone has dived with Scuba breathing apparatus is 332 metres (bear in mind 30 metres is the accepted maximum for recreational divers due to risks of the bends, nitrogen narcosis and oxygen toxicity). The maximum an atmospheric diving suit can possibly reach is 600 metres. The only way people can go deeper than this is within a deep-submergence vehicle (DSV). In 1960 Bathyscaphe Trieste, a DSV, was able to reach Challenger Deep in the Mariana Trench, the world's deepest seabed, at a depth of over 10,900 metres (7 miles) below sea level with 2 people onboard. Can you imagine the amount of pressure that deep underwater? It's the equivalent of about 11 large men trying to stand on the tip of your finger! The walls of this vessel were between 12 and 15cms thick to keep the occupants safe and at normal atmospheric pressure.

ROVs and AUVs are ideal alternatives to be able to explore underwater without risk and at a much-reduced cost compared with building a vessel with a pressure chamber to support human life. Even at shallow depths, perhaps for ship hull inspection or for security patrolling a harbour entry point, ROVs and AUVs are often a better option than divers.

ROVs and AUVs are equipped with video cameras (the eyes of the vehicle) recording or transmitting live video back in the ship so an operator can steer and use the onboard tools. They also need bright lights as it gets darker (and colder) as you descend and there is no natural light after 1000 metres. This also means they can be effective working at night. ROVs more than AUVs can make use of a number of other sensors and attachments to help with their objectives and AUVs though autonomous can be limited to open water, shipping free environments. ROVs are regularly used for deep sea rescue and recovery, one called Argo found the wreck of the Titanic in 1985, though this ROV was towed by a ship, rather than remotely operated. Having manipulator arms with grippers or cutting tools can be useful to work with objects they find underwater, or in case the ROV itself becomes stuck. Both ROVs and AUVs are often used for hydrographic surveying and environmental surveys for offshore and coastal engineering in oil, gas and offshore renewable energy industries, but also for scientific research. ROVs can also help create real-time 3D simulations of underwater environments to be able to analyse an area in more detail than vision alone and also compare a site or asset over time on a computer.

Artificial Intelligence (AI)

So far in this book we have covered different methods of controlling robots and the idea of programming, but what if we were able to programme a robot just once and after that period, it would learn for itself? This is the goal of Artificial General Intelligence (AGI).

Artificial Intelligence is a huge topic that stretches far beyond robotics and has significance for all applications that can be improved by computing intelligence and masses of data – meaning practically everything. AI is already hard at work on our computers, making sense of our browsing history and preferences to select appropriate adverts to show us and also working through our smart speakers, to understand our voice commands and convert these into instructions to switch on a light or find out some online information. These are just a few of the many examples of basic AI in our daily lives. It is the aim of creating artificial life forms - synthetic animals and people - that forms a strong bond between artificial intelligence and robotics. This kind of AI is the ultimate goal of the quest that computing was founded on.

The Turing Test

The emergence of AI methods interlinks the academic work underpinning the development of computing with hypotheses of how our brain uses electricity to function, both with a focus on binary numbers (0 and 1) and symbolic logic. As far back as the 1840s, Lady Ada Lovelace had a notion for basic AI through her work and correspondence with Charles Babbage, the inventor of the first mechanical, digital computer. Lady Lovelace had the vision of a programme that worked on Babbage's Analytical Engine and saw far more potential in computing than just mathematical calculations, though she didn't think that computers could ever be capable of independent learning. It wasn't until Alan Turing developed ideas from his ground breaking work on algorithms and computation within his paper "Computing Machinery and Intelligence" that the idea of artificial intelligence and computers being able to 'take us by surprise' was proposed. He suggested a test called the 'Imitation Game' that had both a human and a computer being asked (written or typed) questions by a human judge, all of whom were in separate rooms. The judge would have to determine which response was human and which was from a computer. If the computer's text-based answers were indistinguishable from a human's, the computer had won and had achieved 'intelligence'. This became known as the 'Turing Test'.

There have been other measures of a computer's 'intelligence' and these have seen a human who is considered the best at something pitted against a computer trained to win at that same game. The company IBM have been heavily involved and successful in these competitions; their chess-playing machine Deep Blue defeated chess champion Garry Kasparov in 1997. After this they developed a very sophisticated supercomputer called IBM Watson who beat the human champions of Jeopardy (a question and answer TV quiz game) in 2011. In order to be successful in this battle with humans, IBM Watson stored millions of pieces of information from encyclopaedias, dictionaries, newspapers and literature and could answer a spoken question within a fraction of a second. This gives you a hint of the amount of information that might be needed for artificial intelligence to satisfy the Turing Test.

> **❝** *Machine learning and AI will empower and improve every business, every government organisation, every philanthropy - basically there's no institution in the world that cannot be improved with machine learning.*
>
> Jeff Bezos, CEO Amazon

> *AI is one of the most important things humanity is working on. It is more profound than ... electricity or fire.*
>
> Sundar Pichai, CEO Google **❞**

> **❝** *Researchers just unveiled a robot that can play scrabble. It's pretty realistic. It even gets bored halfway through and stops playing.*
>
> Comedian Jimmy Fallon, 2018 **❞**

What do we consider natural intelligence to be?

Intelligence is broadly defined as the ability to acquire and apply knowledge and skills. If natural intelligence is a measure of information retained and recalled on request, for example in an exam or perhaps a quiz like Jeopardy, supercomputers already far exceed our capabilities to retain and recall knowledge. The goal of Artificial General Intelligence (AGI, also known as true or strong AI) is to create a computing intelligence (perhaps an algorithm, a programme or a programming language) that provides the behaviours and intelligence equivalent to an animal or human brain. To summarise natural intelligence is quite complicated as it involves cognitive intelligence as well as social and emotional intelligence. Perhaps the key distinction of true intelligence (and true AI) is rather than being fed information, it can seek out and analyse the information for itself, learning social, emotional and factual intelligence independently.

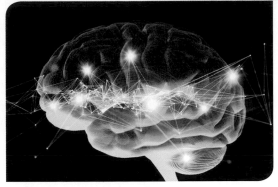

Types of AI

There are multiple sub-segments and related fields to that of Artificial Intelligence, and AI has had an interesting journey of competing and conflicting academic views and directions to become what it is now. These are the two key areas that concern us when designing robotics and androids.

A) Classical or symbolic AI or good old fashioned (GOFAI) also now known as weak AI

- 'Sees' things such as words, 2D or 3D shapes or symbols and associates them with other things

- AI specialism – does one thing or area expertly, also known as connectionism

- E.g., Apple Siri, Amazon Alexa (all voice assistants), Google search, Facebook Advertising etc

- Is based in algorithms and computing, logic that is more easily programmed

B) Artificial General Intelligence – also known as strong or true AI

- Understands the meaning of things and makes use of this understanding

- Self-learning, prediction, anticipation, improvisation; what we might call 'common sense'

- AI generalism – can adapt to a range of topics and skills

- E.g., a truly autonomous robot like C-3PO, breakthroughs are expected within the next 5 years

- Is based in the nuances of learning, not just yes or no, right or wrong

Machine learning and deep learning

Machine Learning (ML) is classical AI put to use with a specific aim of identifying patterns or trends, typically from a large volume of information (e.g., millions of photographs or images) that would make the activity too time consuming for humans to do. ML has become more widely used due to the affordability of data storage and high-speed processing and aims to be able to 'programme' itself. Deep Learning (DL) is a branch of ML focusing on statistics that use software to mimic brain activity based on neural network techniques. The general view is that neither ML nor DL will ever become Artificial General Intelligence.

Neural networks

Another area within AI is that of artificial neural networks. These are computer systems that are inspired by biological neural networks (i.e., human or animal brains). This doesn't mean they are identical to human brains, but they use ideas that follow our understanding of connections in the brain.

> *A robot is a container for AI, sometimes mimicking the human form, sometimes not ... but the AI itself is the computer inside the robot. AI is the brain, and the robot is the body... if it even has a body.*
>
> Tim Urban, 2015

Cognitive robotics

Using a mix of different methods with the aim of achieving the equivalent of Artificial General Intelligence for Robots. The topic sees animal cognition (learning) as its starting point to provide real world skills and learning for robots. We will explore how all these developments might take shape in our view of the future of robotics in the final pages of this book.

Robots Aspiring to be Human

In the first pages of this book, we mentioned that designing a robot to be humanoid wasn't essential and that a robot could be any shape or size. It is also true that being anthropomorphic is less likely to have as much real-world benefit than for example a robotic arm or an autonomous vehicle. Designing a robot to be like a human is full of difficulty; challenges exist in terms of movement, dexterity, balance, co-ordination, and intellect. Things we might consider simple and that young children are capable of doing have taken humanoid robot designers decades to replicate mechanically. The positive thing is, humanity is completely motivated to do this, as the section on science fiction highlighted, we've been attempting to animate human and animal figures for thousands of years. The truth is we now have the technology to make the once crude and often creepy automatons of a few centuries ago much more lifelike. In these pages we look at some of the best simulations of humans to see how far we have come and understand the benefits a life-like humanoid robot might give us.

> *Making realistic robots is going to polarise the market, if you will. You will have some people who love it and some people who will really be disturbed.*
>
> David Hanson, 2006

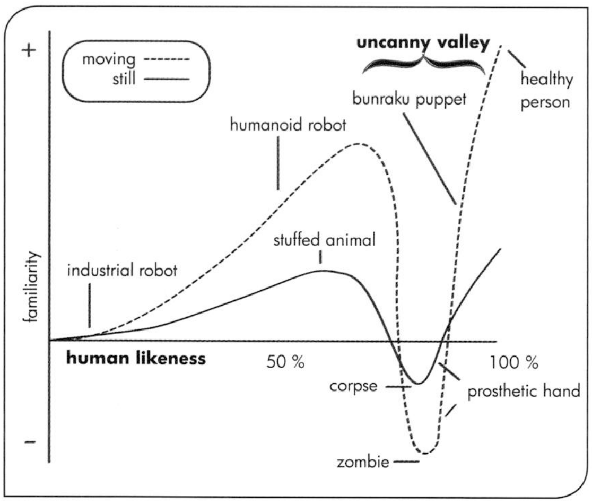

Chart showing human likeness (x-axis) against familiarity (y-axis), with labels: moving (dashed), still (solid), uncanny valley, bunraku puppet, healthy person, humanoid robot, stuffed animal, industrial robot, 50%, 100%, corpse, prosthetic hand, zombie.

Looking like us

A well-known theory about the appearance of humanoid robotics was put forward in 1970 by roboticist Masahiro Mori; he called his concept the uncanny valley. The uncanny valley is based on the idea that if we try to make a robot look human, but it doesn't appear realistic enough, then we find it uncomfortable and creepy to look at or be around. The sensations he witnessed and felt himself have since been tested and found to be generally true.

Mori looked at prosthetic hands and found those that looked realistic at first glance, tended to elicit an undesirable reaction when they moved unrealistically or when people touched them and they didn't feel real. He went on to discuss movement within puppets and dead bodies; when given movement they have the opportunity to freak us out which is exploited by horror film and game creators with zombies. Above left is an image of the uncanny valley chart. As you can see, there are a lot of robotic creations that we feel comfortable with, such as toys and industrial robot manipulators perhaps until they reach over 75% human likeness, at which point we become less at ease. This is borne out when you see videos of humanoid robots not quite smiling correctly, staring for too long and not fixing you with their eyes.

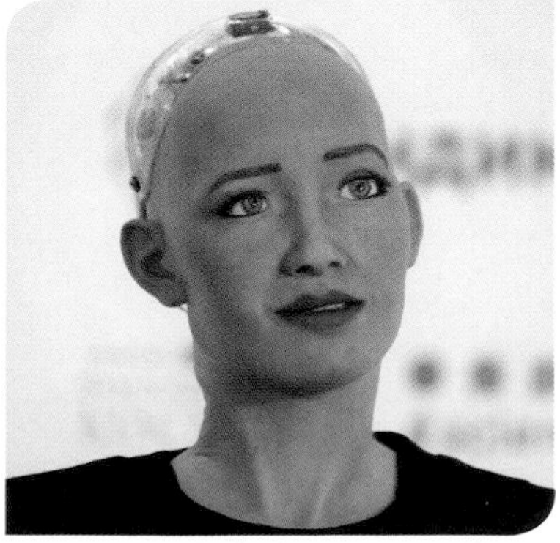

Fifty years later the technology and our craft of creating realism has improved drastically. Skin texture and appearance has become much more like the real thing and we might have our first robot celebrity in the form of Sophia, here, who was developed by Hanson Robotics. With facial features inspired by actress Audrey Hepburn and an artificial intelligence that allows her to competently handle a range of questions and answers when interviewed, she was granted citizenship of Saudi Arabia in 2017 and seems to be getting beyond the uncanny valley (more so when she wears a wig). Sophia works using responses similar to the Artificial Linguistic Internet Chatbot Entity (ALICE) chatbot default responses, which have so far been unable to pass the Turing test, with no judge being fooled into thinking it might be a human. That is not to say that Sophia isn't a fantastic achievement, and just to clarify no-one has yet passed the Turing Test so hopefully this will inspire you to know that there is still work to be done … perhaps you can help make that breakthrough?

Talking like us

The ability for a computer to recognise natural language isn't a new phenomenon; voice has been used to activate toys since 1911 and voice recognition technologies have been attempted since the 1950s. In this period, the technology was predominantly used in research and academic environments, until during the 1990s it made its way into consumer products and some computer and online experiences. Voice assistants weren't generally reliable enough for mainstream use until perfected by Apple in Siri and with versions from Amazon (Alexa) and Google (Assistant) in the past five to ten years they have developed a strong presence in households globally. Social robots tend to have their own voice assistants

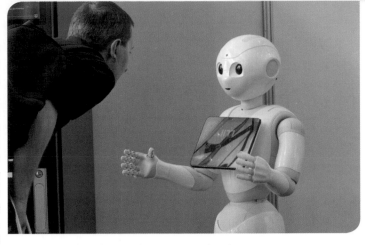

for specific applications around health and wellbeing, particularly for the old. Toys and other consumer robotics have incorporated mainstream voice-assistants; however, none of these kinds of robots are yet in general use in households, but that's not to say there haven't been some great products introduced, and one of these may become a breakthrough for social robotics.

Pepper from Softbank Robotics is a social humanoid robot that has been very successful (with over ten thousand in use) in a mix of academic and real-world applications. Pepper (left) is a child-size robot (1.2m tall), which helps make it approachable and non-threatening. It contains four directional microphones in its head that help it understand the direction of incoming voice and also to interpret emotion. It can recognise speech and dialogue in 15 different languages. It has two HD cameras and a 3D sensor to help it recognise people and movement. The touchscreen tablet gives it wide-ranging applications including customer and visitor information in banks, shops and restaurants and it moves around on concealed wheels.

Walking like us

For mobile robots, having two legs or being bipedal is just one of a number of options for movement; wheels are likely to be an easier method of achieving mobility, but there are advantages in using feet and legs, for example climbing. Walking is one of the first things we humans do to help make the transition between baby and toddler at one or two years of age and after this a world of upright movement opens up to us. The challenge to achieve the required balance for walking, i.e. stable forward motion, has proved a major challenge for roboticists, with some stand-out successes. Honda had a company goal to create a walking robot and started to develop prototypes of ASIMO (picture above) through the 1980s, launching the first version in 2000. ASIMO, which is an acronym of Advanced Step in Innovative Mobility was a great showcase of technological achievement, succeeding in what Honda set out to do – walking (and running) independently, not only this but also the same kind of communication technology and sensors as used by the Pepper robot. Unfortunately, it didn't match its commercial success as a human helper. If there was a title for best walking robot, then in 2013 this was handed from ASIMO to ATLAS (right), from Boston Dynamics - now part of Japanese company Softbank Robotics, who also own the Pepper robot. Atlas was built to help in search and rescue applications and is a very capable all-round robot, as you might expect for use in emergencies. Where it excels is stability over all kinds of terrain: even when pushed or hit with a projectile it can stand on one leg and get up if it falls over, which is well worth seeing in action on YouTube videos.

Robots Inspired by Animals and Nature

Biomimicry or biomimetics is the adoption and imitation of natural life forms as a guide when designing technology solutions and can include any animal or plant system or element. Zoomorphism (meaning 'representing animal forms') and biomimicry have been a significant influence and a positive inspiration for many robotic innovations. Here are some examples of biomimetic and zoomorphic robots.

Four-legged robotic friends

We've seen robotic dogs before in our section on toys and entertainment with interactive pets like the Sony AIBO, which is very capable of mimicking a dog's behaviour. Spot (pictured here) by Boston Dynamics is more like a super dog. On the previous page we highlighted Atlas as a winner at walking. Spot (Mini) has similar skills, but as a quadruped, rather than a biped, finely tuned and perfectly balanced to stand on two of its four legs at a time. As with autonomous vehicles, this kind of high-end robot has abundant sensors and cameras to sense the world around it to avoid obstacles, including people. In order to achieve balance, accelerometers and gyroscopes keep a dynamic view of the moving weight, allowing the limbs to compensate if losing balance and counteract changing stability under its feet. As you might notice in the image, rather than a dog's head, (as Spot doesn't need to look especially cute) it has a robotic arm to help in all manner of uses, such as picking up things and opening doors. Boston Dynamics have created different sized versions of their 4-legged robots to help carry equipment in military scenarios. Elsewhere there are 2-legged (e.g., a jumping kangaroo) 6 and 8-legged (e.g., spider) robots. Another Boston Dynamics' robot 'Handle' - featured earlier in this book - has both legs and wheels for the best of both worlds.

Robotic snakes

These innovations take their inspiration from biological snakes and worms. Though they might look fairly deadly they tend to be used in rescue and medical applications due to their flexibility and ability to move through tight spaces, such as pipes or rubble. Snakes can move over most surfaces, climb and swim by tightening and untightening muscles along their body, moving with an s-shaped motion that when replicated can be used to create an all-terrain 'investigator', such as an infiltrating spy camera or a front-line rescue scout on Earth … or as NASA are planning, an explorer in Space.

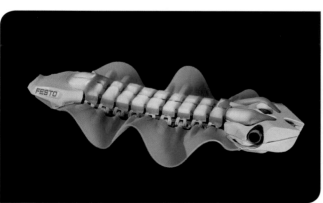

Soft robotics

S-shaped movements also inspired the moving cuttlefish-bot called the BionicFinWave, here. Designed by Festo it has silicone side fins that propel it in any direction. Flexibility in materials and robotic constructions is a key driver for soft robots, with good examples of these being underwater animals such as octopus' tentacles and other invertebrates like worms. Soft robotics is a specific field of robotics that champions biomimicry with the aim of being entirely free of solid components. This discipline in design aims to provide significant advantages in fluidity of movement, energy conservation, adaptation to environments and safety for humans in close proximity. Sometimes soft robotic components can be used in otherwise rigid robots for example to give a soft, flexible arm. In another direction Harvard University created the first autonomous, untethered, soft robot, the Octobot. The Octobot uses flexible components and moves by gas pressures, so avoiding the use of rigid components completely.

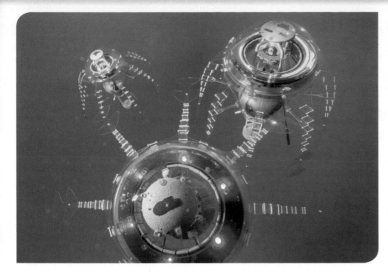

Swimming robots

As we saw in the section on ROVs and UAVs (page 36) there's a whole world of exploration, scientific learning and climate-change tracking to be found underwater. The best method of observing can be to blend with your environment and these AquaJellies from Festo do that by gliding with gentle thrusts through the water, just like jellyfish. This concept had the idea of deploying several jelly fish to monitor water conditions in processing plants in an efficient way providing information to connected smartphone and tablet apps. A radically different need for swimming robots arose after the Fukushima Daiichi nuclear disaster in 2011. The intense levels of radiation following the Level 7 (maximum level) nuclear disaster meant that no human could safely visit the site of the nuclear power plant in Japan, even robots failed to operate on many occasions when tried. The important task ahead is to make the area safe again after 3 nuclear meltdowns and the release of radioactive material during the disaster. This process of decontamination and decommissioning will take between 30 and 40 years. Toshiba has been working with a team of researchers to find a robotic solution to explore flooded parts of the nuclear plant. They created a 'Little Sunfish' ROV powered by 5 propellers that was robust enough to withstand the radiation. Its onboard cameras and radioactive sensors have been able to identify molten nuclear fuel. This will help the next steps of removing the molten metal and radioactive fuel and making the site safe for humans to use again.

Swarm robotics

Much like animals can work seamlessly together to achieve objectives, such as a colony of ants or a swarm of bees prospering through co-operation, this principle has been adopted in swarm robotics.

Swarm robots are different to other multi-robot systems as swarm robots do not have centralised control. Instead, each individual robot is autonomous, with local sensing and communication to other members in the swarm, they can be physically different and perform different roles as happens in a colony or swarm. Multiple, replaceable components in a self-governing system are envisaged in have medical applications, even in minute scale as nanobots, and also in rescue and disaster recovery as well as large area foraging tasks in mining and farming, both on and off our planet. Kilobots (see image) can work in co-ordinated swarms of hundreds of units.

Animal elements

As swarm robotics show, you don't need to copy the whole animal with biomimicry, you can take elements such as behaviours or physical attributes. Robotics has the ability to conjure up a duck-billed platypus of a creation

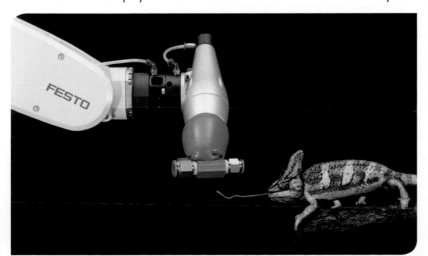

to deliver the right features for the required function. Physical attributes that have been taken from animals include whiskers, like those on rats and cats which allow animals to sense their environment and have been used in Bristol Robotics Lab's Scratchbot. Real world uses might be in rescue scenarios when cameras and other sensors can't be used. Another wonderful natural phenomenon is a chameleon's tongue, which is projected at speed and wraps around unsuspecting insects before delivering a tasty snack. This flexible wrapping technique of the chameleon's tongue has been adopted by Festo in their robotic arm 'FlexShapeGripper' shown here.

The Future of Robotics

A positive force

As you are probably beginning to appreciate, robotics is an exceptionally interesting field of study with an enormous range of applications and potential for our imaginations. The positive achievements that have been made as a result of robotics – including life-saving, planetary and subsea exploration, and impressive factory automation – mean that the potential for good already far outweighs the negative. A recent headline suggested robots would replace 30 million factory jobs by 2030, but in the detail of the study it also stated that this automation will actually increase jobs overall and increase economic growth at the same time.

Science fiction writers have created amazing ideas of what future robots might be able to do, for both good and bad, so much of which seems quite achievable as technology becomes – and we become – more capable. It shouldn't be beyond people your age perhaps fifty years from now to make your own C-3PO, just like Anakin Skywalker did in the Star Wars Episode 1 film. In truth we can get quite close now with the right components, it is really down to you and your desire to be a 'maker' of robotic things.

> **If autonomous robots are going to hang with us, we're going to have to teach them how to behave ... which means finding a way to make them aware of the values that are most important to us**
>
> *Kristen Clark, How to Build a Moral Robot, 2016*

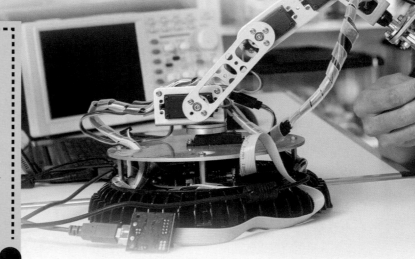

Intelligent

Pursuing intelligence far beyond ours has great potential to allow us to become more advanced than we currently are as we learn from computers and use their abilities to enhance ourselves. Famous people have expressed a fear of AI getting out of hand; both Elon Musk and the late physicist Stephen Hawking expressed serious concerns, as Hawking said "The development of full artificial intelligence could spell the end of the human race." It certainly could, nuclear power also has that capability, but if that is the case, we have failed to safeguard ourselves from our own creation. Humanity has failed. The good thing about robots perhaps is that they will never be human. They won't have the same sometimes ruthless ambition and desire for power that humanity can have, nor a desire to support a team or worship a deity and distrust others who support or worship different ones. They shouldn't be swayed by human weaknesses such as our 7 deadly sins and vices, unless of course we programme them to behave this way.

One thing is certainly clear, the idea that a robot is a machine that blindly follows orders is being challenged: we're driven to make them more sophisticated, to make them think. If you were 'unkindly' calling someone a robot now, it might mean that they were cold and lacked emotion, but this is what scientists are trying to change for robots through AGI, we can give robots ability to react in genuine-seeming emotional ways, like a friend might. When that robot follows Asimov's 3 laws, meaning it is not a threat to us, we should see a future with robots that are near sentient, exhibiting fantastically unique personalities, characters of their own inspired by a mixture of inputs and able to delve into a wealth of knowledge and one liners. They could be be the life and sole of the party.

Better than us?

The problem for us is that robots do have the potential ability to be better than us. They can be stronger, more intelligent, more resilient. This will always make humans fearful, we're only human after all. It is quite possible this will drive our competitive nature and give us opportunity to advance ourselves, augment ourselves with implants and body enhancements. I can't see us wanting to hack body parts off and replace them with bionic ones; though some might, bionic technology has the potential to be wearable, like a super powered onesie we can slip into. But here's what the brilliant mind of Asimov said over 50 years ago:

> *We will have a robot becoming less metal, more organic. At the same time we will have human beings who will make more and more use of artificial organs of metal and plastic, artificial hearts, artificial kidneys, artificial lungs ... replace bones by light metal substitutes ...*
>
> *"In short, we may have a society in which robots will drift away from total metal toward the organic. And human beings will drift away from the total organic toward the metal and plastic. And that somewhere in the middle, they may eventually meet.*
>
> *"When we have a metal/organic hybrid 'creature', will it matter if he was originally metal and became metal/organic or that he was originally organic and became metal/organic. Or will it not matter, will we have formed a mixed culture, which perhaps might be higher, more efficient, better than either 'culture' separately.*
>
> *Isaac Asimov, 1965*

This is definitely an interesting viewpoint and it will be amazing to see how we as a species advance. We have been concerned with the availability of technology through society and the division of wealth, but these kinds of advances have greater potential to widen the gap between the haves and have nots. There are some great science fiction stories and films along these themes, perhaps you can imagine the possibilities yourself?

It's up to you

We should think more about how we treat technology as it becomes more intelligent, perhaps we should be mindful to give it respect. The way we anthropomorphise technology is no bad thing – people naturally work courteously with humanoid robots, treating them as we would people. If a robot is doing all our chores, perhaps we should respect that technology, not make it a cup of tea (as that might not be great for the electronics inside) but at least be appreciative of the freedom that it gives us to do other things. We will see a lot more attempts to create humanoid and other robot companions and this will help inform our view of what we are really looking for in a social robot. It would be wrong not to mention concerns for cyber security, personal safety and privacy; these are genuine worries and will create barriers to us accepting the technology. We can embrace optimism with awareness and caution in order to keep a 'can-do' attitude that there is always a solution to be found that allows progress. At this point in the book, it is well worth thinking of the areas that have been covered and which hold the greatest interest to yourself? Can you see an opportunity to make a difference working with robotics? There will be engineering, commercial and legal matters in focus, in every area of current and future potential use. Good Luck!

> *We're here to put a dent in the universe.*
>
> *Otherwise why else even be here?*
>
> *Steve Jobs*